THE HOW TO MANUAL

A COMPLETE GUIDE TO OWNING AND OPERATING A MASSAGE PARLOR

The Real Story of How to Make a Dream into a Business

Author Gordan Storm
© Copyright 2013

Published Gordan Storm
Blandon, PA 19510

Copies of this book can be ordered from
www.OHCBooks.com/The_Parlor

ISBN-13: 978-1484111178

ISBN-10: 1484111176

TABLE OF CONTENTS

TABLE OF CONTENTS

INTRODUCTION

This "How to Book" is dedicated to all the guys and girls who dream of surrounding themselves with beautiful women and men while making a mountain of money at the same time. **This guide is exactly that, a guide and is not intended as legal advice, direction, or permission to do what is contained within these pages.** As in any business venture you should first research local laws pertaining to this type of business and be able to answer all questions that may arise regarding these legal matters in the locality you are considering operation. The contents of this manual are for the sole purpose of assisting those individuals interested in pursuing this intensely exciting and thoroughly satisfying life style. The pages that follow contain the wealth of knowledge that I have accumulated over the many years of operating my own "club" and turning the dream into a business.

THE AUTHOR AND HIS WIFE

PROLOGUE

My name is Gordan Storm and I was the owner of a very successful "massage parlor" for more than 15 years. The one question I've been asked time and time again is, "HOW DO I GO ABOUT STARTING MY OWN MASSAGE PARLOR". This may seem like a simple enough question, but as you will soon realize it is not a simple one to answer. I am now taking the "HOW DO" question and placing it on paper in this "HOW TO" book. In my case everything came together as I stumbled along making costly mistake after mistake finally working out the winning combinations. This book will help you avoid making those mistakes and accelerate the success of your business.

Before I opened my "club" another "club" was already doing business on the outskirts of my hometown. At that time I operated a swimming pool service company when one day I received a call from a woman claiming she owned a health club that was in need of an immediate service call to repair a whirlpool. When I arrived at the "health club" I was greeted by a very pretty, scantily clad young woman who escorted me passed several more scantily clad women into a windowless room containing a generous amount of mirrors on the walls and one large mirror on the ceiling above the whirlpool.

The repair of the whirlpool required several return calls and in the course of repairing it I got to know several of the girls. At every service call I saw these females parading by me dressed in incredibly revealing attire and I started to ask a lot of questions. The girls were not shy in answering the questions and hearing their answers only increased my curiosity and fascination with what they were doing. Nude massages and then some, hmm, what a thought, what an idea.

One of my concerns was that the total population of the town was somewhere in the neighborhood of 250-300 thousand people. By any standard this is not a large town even though it had several other small communities surrounding it. Could two "health clubs" survive in an area with this limited population? I finally decided there would be only one way to answer the question, open the second club and see the results. This surely was against my normally good business sense but when you weigh business sense against dreams, dreams usually win out.

Over the next few months I couldn't stop thinking about the idea, nude massages and then some, I kept repeating to myself. Although it seemed like a great idea I needed more information and while working at the "health club" I was able to develop a very special relationship with one of the massage girls. While nurturing this special relationship I was able to gain needed information while constantly fantasizing about having my own club. Finally, I started looking for a location and eventually found what I thought to be a suitable site for my own club. The location was a small, boarded up, building at the edge of the city limits tucked away on a side street. In my opinion, who could ask for anything more, out of the way and secluded. To the un-educated eye it looked like a dump but to me it looked a potential palace, the future home of my very own "health club".

The building measured about thirty foot by sixty foot, had two floors, and was in need of major repair. I quickly located the owner and struck up a deal for a three year lease with the option to buy. The owner made clear he had no problem with me gutting the interior and making it into a floor plan that best suited my needs. And with the signing of the lease began the project of converting his dump into my palace.

My special friend from the other "health club" was contributing by quietly recruiting a few of the other girls from that club. They agreed to come and work for me when I was ready to open for business. Besides, promising a management position to my special friend surely helped to secure her loyalty and dedication to my project. In fact, she was so excited with the news that I had signed a lease on a building and anxious to get the club open she began spending all her free time helping with the work needed to finish the project.

The Grand Opening was on a Wednesday at noon with the hours being set as Monday through Saturday noon till midnight. I now had my club manager, two full time girls, and one part time girl to fulfill the needs of my customers. By that Saturday's closing there had been just eighteen customers with gross receipts of $1280.00. Not a landslide start but it was a start. The following week receipts were over $3600.00 and I realized that I was going to need employees to take care of my growing customer base. I placed my first jobs ad and the first week I had forty-two women of varying age show up for interviews.

To help get the word out that we were open for business we

used the newspaper, local community publications, pamphlets and flyers. The girls even went around the parking lots of nightclubs, bars, sport bars and strip clubs leaving flyers about the club on car windshields. Stacks of flyers were also left in the lobbies of motels and hotels, anything to drum up customers.

While concentrating on soliciting business in this manner, the number of employees steadily climbed from four to eight, then 12 in a matter of a few short weeks. Business was increasing rapidly and by end of the first year my small club generated $126,000.00, the following year it more than doubled that amount. It doubled again the year after surpassing the $500,000.00 mark. Every year the customer base kept climbing along with the clubs income and now there was an average of eighteen full-time employees.

After the first year I expanded the hours the club was open to seven days a week. Monday through Thursday the doors stayed open sixteen hours, Friday and Saturday seventeen hours, Sundays eight hours, for those who did and did not attend church. Being opened the eight hours on Sunday proved to be the makings of a very profitable day. By the 11th year sales surpassed the Million Dollar mark and consistently stayed above that well into the 15th year.

Records show that during those fifteen years there had been over two hundred & twenty-five thousand

(225,000) customers who walked through the club's doors and included over twenty-eight thousand (28,000) credit card using customers preferring to pay for our services utilizing that method of payment.

THE LOCATION

The location can be of the utmost importance or of really no significance depending on what side of the business you are looking at it from. From the owner's point of view a location, should be chosen that is easy to find, yet not blatantly exposed so that its presence would bring the unneeded attention of the local moral minority such as being too close to a church, school, or a heavy traffic area such as a shopping mall. It is much more desirable to find a vacant building on the outskirts of town or possibly a side or back street in a commercially zoned or commercial/residential area. The idea being, it's better just to blend in, as low profile is the *key* to longevity.

On the other side of the coin, and from personal experience, customers do not really care where you're located, only the fact that you exist. Of course, there are always the few at first that do not want to be seen entering or leaving your establishment but that usually disappears after the first visit. As long as they have options as to where they can park or they have the cover of darkness whereby a l l o w i n g them to make good use of your evening hours.

THE STRUCTURE

When it comes to the structure's size, size matters only to the extent of the availability to serve your customer base and affordability. A building with as little as fifteen to eighteen hundred square feet can prove to be very profitable, but at the same time leaves little or no room for expansion, should business exceed your expectations.

It is desirable to have at a minimum at least four to five rooms available for your customers. In addition you'll need an office, a front lobby, a dressing room for employees, an employee's lounge, bathrooms, showers, a laundry room, a room for supplies etc. Again the size of the structure is the limiting factor and adequate space should be allotted for the needed areas listed in addition to the customer service areas. The square footage required may be contained in a building that is on a single floor, or with a second floor, but always keep in mind the building's intended use. The intended use of the building is to offer service to your customers in a comfortable, clean, and safe environment.

Try and visualize the possibilities of the structure you are contemplating to transform into your dream *before* laying down cash or signing a lease. If you can't picture your dream in the building you are considering it is probably the wrong building and you should not invest you capital or time into it.

THE INTERIOR

Taking into consideration the need for the different types of rooms described under the heading of Structure it is important to layout the rooms in a manner to allow ease of access for both employees and customers alike. If the building you acquire has an open floor plan, redesigning the layout will be relatively easy. If the building has structural walls or rooms already in existence the redesigning and rebuilding will be more limited and probably more costly. All of these issues are going to affect start-up costs and should be considered before purchasing or leasing a building.

NOTE:

In the appendix of this book I've included several drawings or suggestions for floor plans for both one and two story buildings. These plans can be adjusted accordingly to accommodate your structure and conform to local building codes and regulations. Also, keep in mind the specific needs of your expected customer base.

PLUMBING & ELECTRICAL

It is obvious that the business will need showers, toilets, sinks, washing machines, dryers, hot tub(s) and/or spa(s). All of these need water pipes, drains and other hardware to function properly. When it comes to the plumbing make sure that it is done correctly as there is nothing worse than having plumbing problems during business operation. This is one area to spend extra funds to assure there will be no problems as backed up toilets or showers that do not drain properly will give the image of a dirty facility, **an image you do not want.** Since you'll need to have one or more hot tubs or spas, a clothes dryer and air conditioning, be sure to have adequate electrical service. It is suggested to have at least (200) amp service installed in the building. There should also be multiple outlets in each room for accessories such as a radio, television, lamp(s), etc.

NOTE:
Most spa/hot tubs require 220 volts and a GFI (Ground Fault Interrupter) circuit.
You may also need adequate electric for heating depending on your geographic location. Clothes dryers also require 220 volts as do electric hot water heaters. Note: Many clothes dryers are rated at fifty (50) amps. In the long run choosing a hot water on demand system will prove to be much more cost effective and you'll never run out of hot water. These systems are available across the country and only heat the water as needed. Make sure you follow all state and local building codes as a violation of building codes could cause an interruption in business.

FURNISHINGS

It is best to have a spacious Front lobby but not necessary, although it is more desirable to have a comfortable befitting atmosphere for customers where they are not being crammed in knee to knee with a bunch of other guys. A couple of durable sofas and chairs, coffee tables and a lamp or two will cover the basics for the customer lobby. A few pictures on the wall or maybe a television tuned to a sports channel or as an alternative a music system with low volume music playing. An assortment of magazines distributed about the room and a coffee pot should complete the setting.

The employees lobby should have much the same seating arrangements as the front lobby being capable of music and cable television. This room should have lots of mirrors, chairs and/or vanity tables for the employees to apply makeup. Also consider if the building is large enough, a separate room for changing clothes and applying makeup would be even more beneficial. If the ladies room is large enough it could double for the changing room but again you must visualize the layout to make the best use of the space you have available.

The actual massage rooms should be at least 7' X 11' or larger if possible. The only exception will be the room or rooms with a spa or whirlpool as these should be at least 12' X 15'. The larger the standard rooms are the larger the area for the massage table. It is quite acceptable to build or have built raised platforms approximately 40" tall and wide enough to accept a single size mattress to serve as a massage table.

By building your own tables you can incorporate storage for towels, linens and other needed items utilizing the space underneath each table does wonders for creating much needed storage space.

The alternative is to purchase ordinary single or double beds. For small rooms a day bed works well shoved up against a wall.

Each room should have a small table where powders, oils, lotions, and alcohol can be located. Soft overhead lighting or possibly a dimmer switch is good, although a table lamp does just as good a job. There should be a chair in each room for ease of removing shoes etc. Music is a necessity. Optional items would be a stand, to sit a small television/DVD combo, and an intercom system comes in handy as well.

If at all possible a separate shower for both employee and customer is advisable and may be necessary in locations that require a business license. This also applies to the restrooms. Checking with local zoning and building codes are a must if you are unsure as to how to proceed.

There is a need to allocate space for the storing of supplies to insure no interruptions during business hours. All cleaning supplies, linens, and miscellaneous items should be in adequate supply on the premises at all times.

If you intend to install a whirlpool (highly recommended) it is suggested that you stay with a tub size in the area of 90-120 gallons. This size tub can be filled in about 20 minutes and drained after a single use.

NOTE: Be sure you have adequate water volume and

drainage as the filling and draining of the tub is not only preferred but much more sanitary.

It can be very costly trying to use the same water in the tub day after day, customer after customer, considering the cost of chemicals, and keeping the water hot. Hot tubs and spas also require chemical testing and the labor to monitor the chemistry of the water may get expensive. The labor can be eliminated by draining the tub after each use and wiping it down with a good disinfectant. This takes only minutes to complete and draining and filling the tubs is also much more hygienic.

If space and finances allow it is preferred to have your own laundering capabilities utilizing your employees to operate the washers and dryers. This method not only saves money but speeds things up as compared to having a laundry service picking up and delivering.

A word to the wise on providing handicap access to your business.

Believe it or not there are plenty of the handicaps (physically challenged) out there in want of the services you provide. It would be to your advantage to make every effort to incorporate handicap accessibility where possible.

EQUIPMENT

You may want to create an illusion of sorts depending on your unique requirements. This can be done by purchasing a couple pieces of exercise equipment or a universal gym to occupy a specific area or room. A tanning bed is a l w a y s a nice touch especially for the employees since they'll be spending a lot of sunny days indoors.

In addition to a whirlpool, washer and dryer, etc., other equipment purchases to consider are as follows: televisions, telephones, answering machine, copier, computer, window air conditioners (if the building does not have central air conditioning), calculators, vacuum cleaner, small refrigerator, microwave, DVD players, radios or alternative music source's, coffee pot, surveillance cameras for the front lobby, door chime, file cabinet, safe, office furniture, hot towel racks e t c . Wall to wall carpet is also a good choice.

SUPPLIES

There is no such thing as too much linen i.e., sheets, pillows and pillow cases, hand towels, bath towels, wash cloths.

Then there is the powder, oils, lotions, alcohol, hand sanitizer, hand soap, laundry detergent, bleach, latex gloves, pens, paper, and money envelopes.

Throw rugs should be considered (they offer protection for high traffic areas on wall to wall carpeting).

TELEPHONES

It is recommended that at the very least a two-line phone system be installed, one line for business the other line(s) for private matters. The business line should be dedicated solely for incoming calls and located in the employees lounge. That particular phone should be programmed for no call out capability thus minimizing a busy signal for customers who are calling to inquire as to the hours you are open or possibly to find out what employees might be working that particular shift.

If your finances allow for a Key Phone such as the system Panasonic offers, it is highly recommended. It has a broad range of features that can be programmed to meet your particular needs and can be used as an intercom system as well. As an alternative check with your local phone company and inquire as to what they have available to suit your business needs. The telephone plays an intricate roll and will fast become the lifeline of your business and must be more than adequate to support your customer's needs.

MUSIC

Music is very important, that point can't be stressed enough. It has now become much easier to offer a variety of music in order to satisfy a customer's preference by utilizing a service such as Sirius XM. If finances are tight in the beginning consideration should be given to at least placing a separate music source in each room dedicated to each customer's listening pleasure. (A small portable radio or MP3 player will usually do the trick).

TELEVISIONS

The employee's lounge should have a television to help stave off boredom during the slow times. And again if finances allow, it's a good choice to also install a television in the customer's lounge as it will help keep the customer in the lobby when there is an unusually long wait or if the lobby is crowded.

When a customer is in the lobby you don't want him walking out and a television will help occupy his mind. I've found it to be very successful by installing televisions with DVD combos in customer rooms, often at an additional charge, in order to enjoy *certain* videos with the attendant of his choice.

DECORATING

Customers and employees alike will appreciate rooms that have been decorated with good taste. Since most customers will be male it is a good idea to not go too far to the feminine side when decorating the rooms. Try and vary the color and theme of each room from maybe a rustic or wood cabin look to a modern chrome and glass look. Or if you find yourself under employee pressure to help, you could compromise with a Victorian theme with lots of red and gold or more Asian with black lacquer. Make use of wallpaper, paneling, or even painted walls and murals. A table lamp or two is also a nice touch, maybe throwing in a ceiling fan. If the room has a conventional bed in it, cover the linen with a comforter being sure to remove it before the massage for what should be apparent reasons.

The massage room itself is better suited having wall-to-wall carpeting thus allowing a much quieter atmosphere. Incense is also a good option. It also adds to the decor of the room to hang a painting or two on the walls and as mentioned before music is a must.
 Include a comfortable chair with a nightstand or table preferably o n e w i th a drawer for storage. Assuming there is already a television/DVD in the room the finishing touch could be a heated towel rack and a few men's magazines, maybe an assortment of inexpensive men's cologne for the customer's use.

It cannot be emphasized enough about the importance of mirrors. Use mirrors wherever possible. If the massage table or bed is against the wall or if it is in the corner, line the wall side with mirrors and also the head of the bed. If the bed/table is in the center of the room not near the wall install a huge ceiling mirror directly overhead. You can put mirrors everywhere and the more mirrors the more the affect, customers love the mirrors, all the better to help keep their eyes on their attendant.

NECESSITIES ROOM

Since you will be using some type of platform or bed for the customer to lie on, a mattress is required. A standard bed mattress will fit the bill as it is comfortable and a single size mattress is inexpensive. You will need a mattress for each room. It is suggested that they are fitted with a plastic cover to prevent liquids, oils, and other stains from coming in direct contact with the mattress. Next cover the plastic liner with a fitted sheet. A pillow and pillowcase will be the finishing touch. You may still wish to add a comforter or bedspread but remember to remove it before putting the bed/table to use.

It is a good idea to have at least 3 sheets and 3 pillowcases for quick changes in each room. If your linen is being supplied by an outside vendor or laundry service you may want to increase your standby linens to 6 of each.

Remember to have each massage room supplied with the following items: containers to dispense the massage oil, powder, lotion, diluted alcohol, hand sanitizer, and a box of tissues. In addition a supply of hand and bath towels always keeping in mind that these items should be kept in adequate supply in the storeroom. Your place of business should not only look clean but should be as spotless and germ free as possible. Disinfectants should be used daily throughout the premises and after each massage when the sheets are changed.

There are many spray disinfectants on the market to choose from along with other cleaning products that you may find in any home. Don't forget the tile cleaners for the showers and whirlpool along with Windex for the windows and mirrors.

I've found that once you can demonstrate that you do in fact have a viable business i.e., business cards etc., companies and vendors are more receptive when it comes to extending credit for all your business and purchasing needs.

MARKETING

You'll want to make potential customers aware you are open for business so it is crucial to advertise the opening date and to do so as early as possible. The local newspaper is a good way to get your message out although staying mindful of what you are advertising. The most successful and, both tried and proven method is to have the name of your business end with i.e., spa, salon, or health club. Examples: "Peace of Mind Spa," "Relaxation Salon," "Imperial Health Club," etc. Include in your ad that it is the **Grand opening**, and be sure to list any *specials* you may be offering on that day and your daily specials. List the days and hours you're open for business, your location and phone number. You can enhance your ad by including a photo of a beautiful woman (not nude), maybe one of your employees.

In addition to the newspaper advertisement, smaller local tabloids also work well. Don't pass up any opportunity to get the word out. Print flyers on a computer and distribute the flyers in hotel lobbies that are in the area. Sports bars and men's clubs are a good source of business; their parking lots offer an excellent opportunity for you to slip your flyers under the car's windshield wipers.

You may want to construct a website in addition to the flyers and ads. Chat rooms and blogs can also spread the massage far and wide and don't forget to include Facebook, YouTube, and Tweeter. Use your imagination always being mindful the Internet has undesirable eyes watching also.

POINT OF SALE

NOTE:
As owner, and you happen to be a man, you should consider trying not to be seen by your customers or be heard answering the business telephone. It has been my experience that some customers are easily intimidated by running into another male in the hallway or hearing a MALE VOICE ON THE PHONE WHEN THEY ARE EXPECTING TO HEAR A FEMALE'S VOICE.

If your operation does not have a hostess (which is an option and not necessary) your employees will be handling the collection of the money. Once the customer decides on the length of time he wants to stay, the attendant he has chosen will then show him to the room and at that time collect payment. She then tells him to make himself comfortable and that she'll return in a few minutes after completing the paperwork. Cash is always preferred but other payment methods are gladly accepted i.e., charge cards, traveler's checks, money orders, debit cards, any of which the customer may present instead of cash.
It is not wise to accept personal checks as it is easy for the customer to stop payment or to have the check "bounce". Again, it is STRONGLY recommended that you do not accept personal checks.

AS far as credit cards are concerned you should accept all major cards i.e., Master card, Visa, American Express, Discover, Diners Club, etc., and Debit cards. As your volume of business increases you can bargain with the bank(s) to get a better percentage for what they charge your business for processing the charges made on the card. Check with your local bank or an online bank for a rate that meets your particular requirements. The bank you're doing business with will supply you with a merchant's terminal for processing the cards at the point of sale which your employee will use to verify the funds are available to complete the intended sale. Once the charge goes through the employee then takes the customers card and the charge slip back to the customer for his signature and gives him the customer copy then returns to the office where she then initials the slip. (The employee does this so there is a record of who made the sale).

Note: The only way the Federal Government can get involved with your business (other than the IRS) is through the use of credit card transactions as they represent interstate commerce and come under Federal Law.

This next section of "Point of Sale" deals with what happens to the money once it is collected.

At the beginning of each shift each employee will have what is referred to as a "money envelope." These money envelopes will contain each individual employee's sales (cash& charges) for that particular shift.

Written on each envelope will be the name the employee goes by when working (the name she is known as by customers). Along with this work name she will also write the date of the transaction. This information will be placed on the flap of the envelope.

Running down the length of the envelope the employee will keep a record of her sales for that shift. The time of each sale will be placed on the left side of the envelope and the amount of the sale directly across on the right side.

If the sale was a charge a line should be drawn between the sale amount and the time with the amount of the charged portion of the sale written on this line. It should denote what charge card was used and the card's number.

In certain instances the customer will want to include a tip for his attendant on his charge card resulting in a total charge that does not match any of the offered massage prices. In this case the employee will put the amount of the massage on top of the line shown as sales amount and under the line the amount of tip shown as service charge. By adding these two money amounts together they will equal the amount shown on the right side of the envelope under the sales column.

The reason this is done is to identify the tip to the employee so that it is not mistakenly used as her total of weekly sales which her paycheck is based upon and that it is included and taxed on her paycheck. (After the tip has been taxed the entire amount of the tip is then subtracted from the adjusted net pay amount).

The following is the explanation for the tip being deducted from the employees check.

A big incentive for employees wanting to do this type of work is not only do they have the opportunity to earn a sizable paycheck but also the added benefit of receiving cash daily through tips. Based on over 15 years in the business it has been shown that the average money spent on massages by customers ranges from $90-$120 dollars and of those who spend $90 dollars the average tip is $50 dollars. Another statistic from those 15 years is that if an employee does $2000.00 dollars in sales in any given week the statistics bear out that she would have also received at least one third of that amount again in tips or another $750 + dollars in tips.

Or still another way to look at it is that if the employee is getting 35% of her weekly sales that equates to approximately…$700 dollars based on the $2000 dollars of that week's sale. Add to that the tips for that week of $700 +, that employee's pay would be at least $1400.00 dollars or more that week.

Okay getting back to the tip being deducted from the net pay.

Not every customer has the cash to tip his attendant so he ends up putting the tip on his charge card. Since the tip is put on the charge card it tends to be a larger amount, so even though the charged tip amount will eventually be subjected to tax the larger amount of the tip usually compensates for the amount of tax paid on that tip. In order for the employee to get her charge card tip from that shift she simply retains cash from her envelope in the amount of the charge card tip. If it is done correctly the total amount she collected that day should prove out.

To help prevent mistakes (or employee theft), at least one other employee will count and verify another employee's envelope. If it is determined to be correct the verifying employee will initial the envelope and make sure she witnesses the envelope is sealed and dropped into the safe. The employee drops her own envelope in the safe while the employee who initialed it witnesses it being dropped. Both employees are responsible for the money shown on that envelope.

A petty cash envelope containing $100 - $150 dollars is a necessity for each shift and it is desirable that the cash be in $5.00's.

Petty cash is there for the sole purpose of making change for the customer that requires change from large bills. The petty cash envelope should be counted by each employee coming on and going off the shift. Everyone then initials the envelope. If petty is found to be short, each employee will contribute the amount of the shortage thus ensuring the employee responsible for the missing money is among the group that initialed the envelope attesting to it being correct and each person who initialed the envelope replaced what money was missing. Doing this is the only way to be certain the employee who made the mistake and/or the employee who pocketed the missing money does not win. If $5.00 is missing each employee will put $5.00 into individual envelopes and drop them in the safe. If one takes money all pay it back.

Employees attempting to convert their charged tips to cash can, if necessary, join their envelopes together at the end of the shift to successfully retrieve their tip by using each other's charges and cash to work it out as long as their joined envelopes equal the total of recorded sales added together, that is to say their combined envelopes **must** match the total sales for that shift.

Following is an explanation of a White Sheet:

The White Sheet is the daily shift record of the types of massages that were performed on that particular shift, the total of massages, and which employee provided the services. There are a minimum of two white sheets used each day or at the minimum one for each shift. If more space is needed due to an exceptionally busy shift, a second or even a third sheet may be required. Therefore it is a good idea to have a stockpile of white sheets on hand at all times.

The White Sheet is made up as a grid resembling a "computer spreadsheet" similar to those found in Microsoft Excel.

At the very top of the White Sheet there should be a place for the dates from the beginning of the workweek to the end of the workweek. Below is the grid with at least 20 horizontal lines to record, the massage information. The number of vertical lines will depend on how much information you require.

An example would be a column for the attendant's name, type of massage, method of payment, time of the massage, cost of massage, etc.

As each attendant gets a customer she will record the required information on the white sheet as well as on her money envelope before she begins the massage. At the end of each shift the white sheet is then dropped into the safe along with all employees envelopes for that shift. At the change of shifts a new white sheet is put into service for the next shift.

Petty cash is then counted by all employees leaving and by all employees coming on shift.

Only when petty cash is found to be correct all employees from both shifts will then initial the envelope.

Note: A word about the safe.

Without a doubt the best way to secure your hard-earned money is to install an in floor safe, preferably in a cement floor. (Starr Industries is a good choice for a safe.) It will be next to impossible for a would-be thief to bust this safe out of the floor or for that matter to bust into it. If you have a wooden floor it is suggested you get a high quality and heavy floor safe with an electronic keypad or a key/combination lock. If the safe you've chosen is not very heavy it would be wise to bolt it to the floor. Have holes drilled through the bottom of the safe and through the floor. Install washers and bolts followed by tightening the nuts securely finishing the installation by rounding off the nuts so they cannot be removed. **It's your money, <u>you</u> must protect it!**

The information just detailed about the white sheet and safe is of the utmost importance. Sooner or later you will end up with an employee(s) who will steal money and the white sheets will leave a trail to the thief. Remember, a bad employee(s) can come up with some very inventive and ingenious ways to get around your safe guards.

Also there are the disgruntle customers and the terminated employee who had a boyfriend she has given "inside" information to and your business then becomes an easy target. Remember an ounce of prevention goes a long way in limiting the problems that go along with any business.

*An example of a white sheet and a money envelope are ncluded in the back of this book for your convenience.

BOOKKEEPING

When dealing with a large amount of cash, as you will in this business, it is best (at least at first) to count the cash and other forms of payment yourself. You must determine when the end of your business week will be in order to come up with a total of sales for the week.

After you have collected all the employee's money envelopes for the week along with the week's white sheets it is time to compare the totals.
 Take each employee's envelope one day at a time for the day and night shifts and match them with the corresponding sales on the white sheet for that particular shift. Check it off both on the white sheet and the envelope placing each off to the side, white sheet on one stack and each employee's envelopes on their own separate stacks. Do this for the entire workweek, every week.

After having **every** employee's envelopes stacked side by-side, the next step is to total each of the employee's envelopes to get a total for service sales for the week. Once all the envelopes have been totaled separately you must now combine all the envelopes to come up with the total of sales for the week. This total is now compared to the total you arrived at by using the white sheet information.

Using the before mentioned information it should now match up to a personal work sheet grid you keep safely away from all employees. This personal grid is a simple list indicating the name of the employee (work name) down the sheet while having the days of the week across the sheet. The last line down is for that days total and the last column over represents the employee's total sales for the week. At the far right bottom where the total of the days are listed from left to right and the employees totals are listed from top to bottom there should be a matching total.

(An example of this personal grid is included in the back of this book).

If the totals from each sheet do not match, simply compare the envelopes against the white sheet to locate the discrepancy. After all is proven to be correct it is now time to open the envelopes and compare its content to what is recorded by the employee on the outside of the envelope. If the envelope is short any amount of cash the employee is notified and it will be deducted from her paycheck. If the amount the envelope is short matches that of a massage, that amount will then be deducted from her paycheck along with the employee not receiving credit on her weekly sales total that is used to determine her pay for that week.

NOTE: (This procedure is necessary to discourage theft and should be clearly stated in the employee's manual/handbook).

Rather than paying employees strictly an hourly wage it is

better to give her an incentive to do her best and the way to do that is to pay her commission on her weekly sales.

A fair range to offer is 25%-40% based upon performance or you may wish to offer a sliding percentage based on the amount of her sales for the week.

As your business grows so will your employees income. It is not unusual for an employee to go home each shift with well over a $200.00 dollars in tips alone.

Employees by law must pay tax on all money earned including tips. All tips on charge will be claimed and added to the employees pay earned by commission. That tip will then be taxed as ordinary income, and then the entire amount of the tip on charge will be deducted from her net pay because she would have already during the course of the week exchanged that charged tip for cash from her envelope or from another employee's envelope.

Note: Tips on charge are automatically calculated and taxed by the employer. **Cash tips are the responsibility of the employee to declare.**

The bank you do your business with will provide you with a business checking account along with payroll checks or you can do your own thing with the payroll and checks by computer or Internet. One suggestion is Quick Books Pro as it contains most of the features needed to operate a small business.

It may also be prudent to use another title or name for the header on the payroll check. Some employees prefer not to have others know where they work. It is advisable to set your business up as a corporation using a DBA (doing business as) for your actual business site. i.e., ABC Inc. (dba) Piece of Mind Spa. The Corporation name, ABC Inc. is the *only* name appearing on the check.

HIRING

When I first started my business I took advantage of an existing business, and it was the only business of its type at that time in town. It was on a visit to that business which actually gave me the idea that I could do this. I eventually ended up convincing a few of their employees to come and work at my club. There is no denying the advantage to using that method, but it's also dependent on the existence of a similar business in your area. Word has a way of getting around if you are the new club opening up. If that's the situation it will attract customers and potential employees who were both customer and employee at an already established business. Having said that, and assuming you aren't lucky enough to hire experienced employees, you'll start advertising using every source imaginable i.e., newspapers, tabloids, local publications, and the Internet.

The most successful ad will state that you're looking for a "Health Club Attendant," or persons wanted for training as a health club attendant, or experienced health club attendant or persons willing to learn the art of massage. Offer an attractive hourly rate while in training along with opportunities to earn commissions. As your business grows you can also include in your ad's benefits such as paid vacation, holidays, medical etc. You will need to have a female to help run the day-to-day operation and most importantly to help train the new employees. So it is a good idea when conducting interviews to be alert as to who may be interested, and to who you might think would be a potential candidate for your all-important club manager.

Choosing a manager as soon as possible is vitally important. This is a woman you'll be spending a lot of time with thoroughly explaining the entire concept of your business and what you require of her as your manager, which among other things would include the hiring and firing of employees and their proper training.

Having a female as manager makes it much easier to get your point across "girl to girl". It takes a lot of practice as a man to convey to a woman all the intimacies that comes with the job. One woman speaking to another woman accomplishes this simply in a relaxed manner in general conversation. Do not be surprised if one out of five just decides to walk away, sometimes even before the interview. Three out of five will say they'll take the job and one out of those three will actually show up for training. Bear in mind, you will not want to hire everyone who shows up for the interviews. Simply some will not be masseuse material, i.e., appearance, weight, etc. The best way to handle those situations is to tell them the positions have been filled at this time and you will keep their application on file and notify them should another position becomes available. If a male applies simply tell him that the male position has been filled. Some media sources give you a hassle if you attempt to run help wanted ads based on a single gender. To get around this problem run your ad "masseur/masseuse".

NOTE: There is no accounting for taste. Just because you may find an applicant unappealing doesn't mean your customers will see her in the same light. Hire a variety of the female species and see what your customers like.

ROLL OF THE EMPLOYEE

The foremost roll of the employee is to greet the customer and explain to him the services that your business provides which includes but is not limited to the prices of the different massages and their length of time and any specials or promotions that are currently being offered. The employee is to do this in a courteous and professional manner. As a side note, most customers are well behaved, while at times some can be rude and maybe intoxicated. It is of the utmost importance that the employee remains in control and always remains a "lady". If the customer would like to meet any of the other attendants that are available she should smile and tell him that she will go and have whoever is available to come and introduce herself.

If on the other hand you have a hostess whose sole job is to greet the customer she will be the one who shows him in and explains to him what is described above and makes sure he meets all available attendants who are on duty.

Once the customer has chosen his attendant and the length of his massage he is shown to the designated room at which time payment is collected. The attendant then excuses herself to complete the paperwork and as she leaves asks the customer to make himself comfortable and she will return in a few minutes to begin the massage. Above all the employee should do her very best to give the customer every reason to visit your establishment again and again.

As an alternative to the previous paragraph you may want to instead have the attendant show the customer to a changing room your establishment has outfitted with lockers, mirrors, benches and/or chairs, possibly a shower and restroom (optional). After having placed his clothes and valuables into his secure locker he would then put on a clean robe provided by you and upon the return of his attendant he can then be escorted to the room chosen for the massage.

Note:
Management may at its discretion assign other duties to employees as deemed appropriate in certain situations. Remember, it is your business and you must always maintain control and job assignments are a form of Control.

TRAINING

As can be imagined proper training is crucial to your business due to the intimacies, safety, and legalities of the job. An employee must fully appreciate the situation she is in every time she enters a massage. She is wearing little or no clothing in the average massage and if it goes as it should the customer should be totally satisfied and feel he had a pleasant, memorable time, with the attendant of his choice.

On the rare occasion a customer becomes hard to handle or rude, remember his attendant is nude or semi-nude and this can make for an uncomfortable situation, endanger the attendant's safety, and lead to possible legal ramifications. The training of your employees must cover every possible scenario that could present itself in a massage and how to handle each scenario.

Training starts with verbal instructions between the employee and her manager. This instruction will cover everything from greeting the customer, the massage itself, and escorting the customer to the door when it is time to leave. The trainee will be taught attendants etiquette, personal hygiene, what outfits/clothing can be worn, even a lesson on the proper use of cosmetics. After the verbal instruction it is preferable for the trainee to accompany her manager into an actual massage or if that is not possible she should at least do a few massages together with other experienced employees in order to become familiar with and participate in the techniques as applied in the different types and lengths of massages.

If in the beginning you do not have a manager to work with the trainees, you must improvise and avail yourself as a stand in customer for training purposes with the first employee you hire. Since you will be training this employee directly she would be the logical chose for your manager.

The trainee must get past any inhibitions about being nude or semi-nude or being in contact with a nude or semi-nude customer. It should be thoroughly understood by the trainee that the massages being offered are full body massages where the attendant massages the customer and the customer is offered the opportunity to massage the attendant and the total experience is to be a sensual one without any illegal activities.

It is well advised to have posted throughout your establishment signs informing the customers there is no sex offered or permitted and that no attendant will perform any illegal act(s). In addition this notice should also inform the customer that once the massage begins there will be no refunds, no exceptions, and if for any reason you our valued customer feels you have not been treated fairly please bring it to the manager's attention.

If during the massage the customer, gets pushy or rough although not to the point where the attendant feels threatened she should calmly state the following "now why don't you just behave and we can continue having a nice time, but if you continue acting badly I will have no choice but to end the massage and leave you all alone to deal with yourself for the remainder of your time."

Once the massage begins and for some reason the customer and the attendant just can't get along and the massage is less than half over, under most circumstances the customer should be offered the opportunity to spend his remaining time with a different attendant of his choice.

If this offer is not satisfactory with the customer, management and management alone, at her discretion, could offer him a massage at no cost to him on a future visit. Under no circumstances will there be a refund.

If the attendant is asked by the customer to refund his payment she will respond by saying that it was impossible since it is policy to drop all monies into the safe as soon as it is taken to the office. The same answer is to be given if she is asked to return the tip.

Keeping in mind the aforementioned, without the customer there is no business. The very reason your business exists is to make money, and to make money you must continue to have satisfied customers. First and foremost you must gear your business to be willing to go to great lengths to ensure your customers have a pleasant and memorable experience, an experience he will want to relive again and again. Your establishment must continue to provide this level of service while maintaining the integrity of the rules on which you operate.

Offering the customer a broad range of prices is accomplished by having several different massages determined by the length of time purchased by the customer, ie: 15 minute, 20 minute, 30 minute 40 minute 45 minute 60 minute, and a 90 minute. Whereas the 60 & 90 minute usually include the whirlpool.

The 15-minute massage being a basic massage (fully

clothed), and then there remains a 20-minute massage, that being a topless massage. These last two I've mentioned are not mutual massages, (mutual massage is a massage where both the attendant and the customer have the opportunity to massage each other).

An example of a 30-minute mutual massage would be with the customer lying on his stomach while his attendant massages his back for the first 5 minutes. Then his attendant would switch places with him and her customer would then massage her back for the next 5 minutes. Then they would switch places again this time with her customer lying on his back again for another 5 minutes followed by yet another switch with his attendant on her back. Once the last 5 minute position is over the customer would then have the massage continued till the end of the time he purchased either lying on his stomach or back whichever he prefers.

In order to avoid the possibility of compromising positions the attendant should always be aware of body positioning. The easiest way to avoid potentially awkward moments is for the attendant never to allow the customers two legs between her two legs or to allow him to man handle her body in such a way as to allow herself to be put into a position where she could be readily compromised into facilitating an illegal act. **Penetration no matter how slight is illegal and the attendant is to make sure that her customer is absolutely made aware of that fact and that under no circumstances will it be permitted or tolerated.**

There are many varieties of powders, lotions, and oils available to make the massage more enjoyable. The attendant should be sure there is alcohol (diluted with water) present to help clean up any excess oil used during the massage.

After having concluded the massage and before excusing herself she should offer the customer a hand towel, a heated one if it is available and then say that she will return in a few minutes to escort him out. If the customer is not yet getting dressed when she leaves the room she should quickly take a rinse off shower, get dressed and return to the room or if the customer was in a hurry to leave she should forgo the shower and wait a few minutes then return to the room and escort him out politely always with a smile on her face.

Then the attendant shall return to the room and remove the sheets and pillowcase to be laundered replacing them with clean linens. Lastly tidy up the room by making sure there are no smudges on the mirrors etc. and refill the oil, powder, and lotions. It is a nice touch to spray a fragrance in the room so that not only is the room neat and presentable but smells clean for the next customer, then follow up with a shower if the attendant has not already done so.

Note: It is a good practice to evaluate employees performance ever so often to be sure no bad habits have developed and they are performing the massages as they were instructed.

It has been my experience that you should always be hiring. If you're lucky, you'll have a few employees who will stay with you for years, and a higher number that will be there only a few weeks to a few months. But that's okay. The reason it's okay is the employees that are with you for a long time are there for a reason. They do a good job and by doing a good job they have repeat customers or (regulars) as the employees refer to them. But it's okay about the short-term employees also. Men like variety and the turnover of some of the employees every ninety days or so only ensure that the discriminating customer will continue to showing up at your door.

On the average the customer returns at least once every ten days, but there are those who return every few days or stay the same day for several massages or attendants.

CLOTHING

The color red is by far the most popular color according to customer preference. During the fifteen years of operation in this business more attendants are chosen when wearing the color red especially in the evening hours, Saturday night in particular. Having said that, what your employee wears will have a direct impact on her success and on your business. It cannot be stressed enough that no matter what she wears it must always be clean, with no holes and no wrinkles. The usual attire or outfit worn would be something on the order of a two piece swimsuit or bikini, maybe lingerie, or intimate apparel such as bra and panties, a garter belt and stockings, or some other form of outfit that this particular employee can pull off as being sexy.

Special requests by customers often involve roll playing and the attendant to be dressed as a nurse, secretary, a schoolgirl, a French maid, leather & lace, dominatrix, and many more left to the imagination. Whenever possible whatever is worn can always be complimented by the attendant wearing sheer to the waist pantyhose. Pantyhose make average legs look good, and good legs are made to look great and add a touch of class to certain outfits. My success through fifteen years was almost entirely due to running the business in a manner in which the cleanliness of the rooms and the class act of the attendants continued to be far and above any of the competition. **"A clean club has class"**. A high standard must be implemented and maintained and it must not be compromised. You must insist that your employees perform at their highest level when with, or greeting a customer.

EMPLOYEE EDIQUETTE

There can never be enough said as to how the employee conducts herself in the presence of the customer. Bad days and personal problems cannot interfere. An employee has the responsibility to appear as the perfect attendant at all phases of the massage process. For the employees who smoke it should only be done in a designated area such as the ladies room and should not be permitted in the massage rooms by either the employee or the customer, if for no other reason than fire safety. The attendant who smokes should always use a breath mint rather than during the massage chewing a stick of gum (chewing gum does not appear lady like). It is preferred that she wash her hands when finished smoking. The attendant must keep up the appearance of being happy even if she for some reason or other is not, always greeting the customer with a smile on her face and maintaining her professionalism and be ever the **"lady"** even when the customer behaves rudely.

Tipping is appreciated but not necessary and a sign stating this should be posted throughout the premises. Having said that, there will be times that a tip is inferred by the customer but when it's time to leave the tip is not forthcoming as the attendant had the right to expect. If this happens there are several ways to handle the situation, always being the professional, "the lady". The attendant would say, "didn't I understand you to say that you were going to show me your appreciation for a having an enjoyable time with me? I thought we had a nice time didn't you", all the while putting a hurt look on her face.

If the above example doesn't bring out the tip, she should let it go and escort him to the door. There have been uncountable times when the customer waits till he's at the door before he hands over the tip. At this point if there is still no promised tip the attendant, still the lady, again says she hopes he enjoyed himself as she had and that he visits again.

Under no circumstances should she raise her voice or lose her composure in anyway. A customer who promises a tip for extra special treatment, to which he is then treated, and then fails in his word to give the tip he suggested he would be better dealt when next he returns. When this happens and he requests the same attendant she may then remind him of his previous visit and give him that moment to make up for his past behavior, all the while she is fully composed. If the customer wants to play dumb, as some do, the attendant whom he had taken advantage of previously can exact her revenge by politely refusing a massage with him and suggest that he meet the other attendants that are available.

By this time the word has spread. Although it is understood and perfectly acceptable for a customer not to tip it is a different story when one is inferred or promised and is not given. No matter what the outcome the attendant will always behave in a lady like professional manner.

EMPLOYEE HYGIENE

When oil and/or powder is used during a massage invariably the attendant will end up with either oil or powder, sometimes both, on parts of her body which is in and by itself justification for at least a rinse off shower before getting dressed and ready to greet the next customer. A bad impression is sent when an attendant disrobes with her next customer and has visible oil smears or patches of powder on her body. That will be a big turn off to most men and should never happen. It is also good practice to begin every massage with both the attendant and the customer making use of the hand sanitizer for fifteen seconds as this hand cleaning goes a long way in the preventing of germs.

To accomplish this, the attendant should nonchalantly pick up the container of sanitizer and squirt a small amount on her hands as well as the customers saying something like "now we both have squeaky clean hands." Doing this should appear to be simply routine. If the attendant somehow determines the customer is definitely in need of a shower, she should offer it to him or maybe suggest they shower together in order to keep him from being offended or embarrassed.

If he is filthy he may be refused the massage or the attendant may choose to avoid a hassle by instead before entering the massage simply put a small dab of perfume under her nose rather than insulting him. The guy just might be a huge tipper. It would be remiss not to mention that all employees keep their underarms and legs free of body hair and advised they should also keep their pubic area trimmed neatly bikini style or something similar not only for appearance but more importantly it is good hygiene.

COSMETIC'S, BODY PIERCING, AND TATTOOS

All women love cosmetics, lipstick, eye shadow, and especially perfume. There are several things to consider while working in this unique environment. Consideration must be given to the fact that the majority of customers will be men. One thing to remember is that many of them are married, or have girlfriends.

It is best for the attendant to use her perfume sparingly as well as her lipstick. Too much perfume carried home or lipstick on his collar could prove to be a big problem to explain to his significant other. This could be a big enough problem that he may never return to your establishment. So the end result of using too much perfume and lipstick is a loss of a customer. Another reason to consider the amount of perfume and lipstick is the customer may not choose this particular attendant if he feels she's wearing the perfume or lipstick too heavy for him to risk carrying a trace of it home. In that particular instance the attendant will never know the reason she wasn't chosen. The attendant should also keep in mind that she is working in a low light atmosphere and it will be much harder for the customer to spot those tiny imperfections she is so worried about.

In so far as body piercing and tattoos are concerned they should be evaluated at the initial interview. Ear, tongue, and vaginal piercing are rarely a concern. Whereas facial piercing such as nose and eyebrow will usually dictate the amount of business an employee is able to procure. All of the above must be determined on an individual basis by management.

CERTIFICATION

During the course of operating your business you may want to have at least some of your employees take classes in therapeutic and/or reflexology and be certified in these types of massage therapy, or choose other forms of massage when training is available in your area. Being able to demonstrate that you have employees with specialized training and are certified could be of help to your standing in the community as a credible business.

DRUG TESTING

The very nature of this type of business lends itself to having hired an employee(s) who have a possible drug abuse issue. Drug use has no place in the work environment and should not be tolerated. If your business demands zero tolerance then there must be a mandatory drug testing policy. Testing should be done randomly with all employees and be part of the employees manual and/or employees contract.

HOLIDAYS

From the employee's viewpoint a holiday is a day off from work, or at least the major holidays should be a day off from work. From the customer's point of view it is a day your business is more than likely closed.

Within the first year of my business being open I learned that if your doors were open, they will come. This fact was discovered after having listened to the business's answering machine upon returning to the office following a holiday. There were numerous messages left inquiring as to whether or not we were open that day. Now armed with this information I instituted the practice of staying open on holidays for a reduced number of hours and only if at least two or three employees volunteered to work that day. Around the same time I expanded the normal business hours from twelve hours a day to sixteen hours a day, seventeen hours on Friday and Saturday, and eventually opened on Sunday for ten hours.

The premise behind these expanded hours and Sunday is that there are enough customers out there who, for no other reason than there being lonely, find it very comforting to have somewhere to go regardless of the hour or day where they can spend a pleasant time, a nice alternative to otherwise being alone on that special day.

EMPLOYEE CONTRACT AND MANUAL

It is your business and you alone must decide to have a written set of rules. Having rules is a wise decision. This can be accomplished by utilizing an employee contract, an employee manual or both. The employee contract should be read and signed at the time the employee is hired. It should state the terms and conditions under which the employee is hired, rate of pay, whether it is hourly, commission, or both. If commission, state the percentage, shift hours, duties and requirements of the employee. You should also have an employee's photo included in the employee file along with a valid Id and date of birth.

The employee manual should not only be a guide that covers things in the employee contract but a source of information on how the business operates. **There needs to be some language concerning illegal acts and that they are not tolerated, and will result in immediate dismissal**. A section covering vacations, holidays, medical coverage, etc. must also be included. How the pay is determined and when they are paid. A section on acceptable clothing, hygiene, etiquette, and a section discussing infractions and or serious violations of company policy and what disciplinary actions are taken due to the degree of severity of the violation for the particular offense. Lastly, the manual must include an explanation as to the roll of the employee in relationship with management.

BUSINESS HOURS

The hours your business is opened will depend on several factors. These factors consist of your location, the number of employees you have and your customer flow.

In the first weeks and months of your being open the flow of customers and the number of employees you have will dictate how long you keep the doors open. It is unrealistic to expect two to three employees to stay at work twelve hours or more a day or to be open that amount of hours when the number of customers coming through the door do not justify it.

If your business is located in a somewhat isolated area it may take some time to establish yourself. Word of mouth will soon get around through your customers and **continuous advertising** in all available sources will assist in making your existence known. In the beginning keep your hours in line with the customers you have and the amount of attendants available for them. You can always expand your hours as your customers grow along with expanding your staff. In my way of thinking it is good idea to have as many employees as possible, the sooner the better. The point being is, the more attendants you have for a customer to choose from the more customers will visit your establishment. There is nothing better for the customer when calling to hear four, five or six names being mentioned representing the number of attendants to choose from when he walks through your door.

Note: Never let the employee dictate to you that there are too many attendants on shift for her to make any money. The more names the customer hears over the phone the higher the chances he will be visiting your establishment. The above is **a time-tested fact** and the way to do business in this profession.

DISCOUNTS & SPECIALS

Discounts and Specials are not only profitable but necessary in the sense that they are helpful in attracting the potential customer who is always looking for a bargain, while at the same time it is also a way of rewarding the repeat customer or as the employees tend to refer to them as their "regulars."

If you decide to call your business a "club" there is an advantage to doing so. Now the customer has a chance of becoming a member of your club, which from time to time entitles him to membership discounts etc. This will also make him feel that he has an advantage over the non-member.

Note: The following is an explanation of becoming a member;

1) When a first time customer visits your club he is told of the services you provide (massages, etc.), the length of time and cost.

2) Explain to the customer that he can become a member of your establishment thereby being eligible for all membership specials that your establishment offers. Most men coming through your door will choose to stay a half hour or longer. What you've accomplished by this is that the customer may purchase a higher priced massage, and becoming a member of your exclusive club, he now feels privileged, good about himself..."special".

Handing out a non-descript membership card to each new customer will have its advantages. One of them being, now the customer has a card showing he is a member of your club and he can now show the card and brag about it to all his male friends which will inevitably become more business through your door.

As the card-holding member r e v i s i t s your club you will be able to recognize some of his preferences. These may include his likes and dislikes, and what attendants he spends most of his visits with. This also allows the keeping of a casual record of how many times he has visited and using that information you can offer him a membership discount upon reaching a pre- determined number of visits.

The bargain hunting customer is drawn to your establishment because of the advertised special for a given day, such as new member discounts. You can advertise these discounts and/or specials in your ongoing newspaper ad or over the telephone as they call in to find out about your services or the attendants who might be working that shift. It is a good practice not to give a customer too much information over the telephone, as it is far better to have them curious enough to stop by in person. It is considerably easier to get a customer to stay once he is there speaking face to face with one of your attendants. Keep in mind that all specials do not have to consist of or be solely based on money. Imagination is your only limitation, i.e. two attendants for the price of one.

CUSTOMER REQUESTS & PURCHASES

You will find as owner of this business there are some very strange people out there, and that they come up with some wild requests. Of course your living is based on customers and their being satisfied with the service your business provides. But remember, in this type of business the customer is not always right.

Prohibiting requests that are illegal or requests that could be considered to be illegal is good business policy, but always strive to do your best to honor the customer's request whenever possible. Good judgment on the part of management will keep your regrets to a minimum. Keep a supply of costumes on hand for those customers who like roll playing and remember there are those customers who love to be dominated, Leather, Whips, Handcuffs, Leash, Paddles, etc.

Then there are those customers who demonstrate a particular interest in some articles of clothing the attendant had been wearing and would like to obtain it by offering to purchase it. Years of experience have shown that to offer for sale or have up for bidding previously worn attendants articles of clothing will satisfy those customers with that special need and generate a degree of enjoyment for your employees. Simply display these articles on a wall or in a display case in plain view of the customer. The bottom line to a successful business is to outperform your competitor by being constantly aware of the customer's needs and wants. Providing the customer's needs and wants in a professional manner, one that displays to the customer your willingness to go that extra mile to keep him coming back for more is a winning combination.

COMPETITION AND THE ECONOMY

Competition not only increases the quality of your business but it also increases the quantity of your business.

When my business first opened there had been only one similar establishment in the entire county. Over the years the number increased to six and then to seven, some of them being as close as two miles away. With that increase of competitors along with it followed an increased awareness to the potential customers that places like this actually exist. Word seemed to spread quickly and my club saw a marked increase in the flow of customers that could only be contributed to word of mouth and to the fact that my competitors were advertising side by side with my ads in the newspapers (Ad grouping).

Another way to stay ahead of the competition is to visit their establishments unbeknownst to them as a customer. Take a look around, see what they are doing, and see how they are running things. They may be offering what is referred to as a "Table Shower", something I never thought of as appealing or profitable considering the expense and the space required for that special type room. And then on the other hand a table shower can play another roll by being a facade of sorts if you feel a facade is necessary. In either case, visiting competitor's establishments will give you valuable heads up on what your competition is doing.

In the entire time my club was in business sales **never** appeared to be tied to the state of the economy. Owning and operating a " Massage Parlor " was then, and is still today, arguably one of the best and most profitable businesses to be involved in, good economy or bad.

A man above all craves female companionship, and the closer this female companionship comes to the sexual end of the scale the more a man's animal instincts take over. Customers will always find the means to come to your establishment in order to spend an enjoyable relaxing carefree time with a beautiful woman, and that's what it's all about. **BUILD IT AND THEY WILL COME.**

EPILOGUE

Now that you have read this How to Manual and have gained the necessary knowledge to go forward with your very own "Health club ", what are you going to do about it?

If you already have a source of disposable income you're half way to achieving your dream. There is simply no reason to put it off any longer. **Just dive in, it is a win, win situation.** And if your available cash is limited or not that forthcoming, it really doesn't take an arm and a leg to get started. My initial investment was approximately twelve thousand dollars, not a big investment for the millions in return.

And for those of you who still might be skeptical, I didn't have the advantage of a book explaining every detail on how to do it. Again, and this cannot be stressed enough, this How to Manual will be the most valuable tool in your possession. Make use of this tool, you have everything to gain. After all, this is the beginning of your new life, and it's going to be a great one!

Be sure to watch for the upcoming book "Curiosities", it is the real life story of the very club this How to Manual is based on.

APPENDIX

SAMPLE FLOOR

PLANS

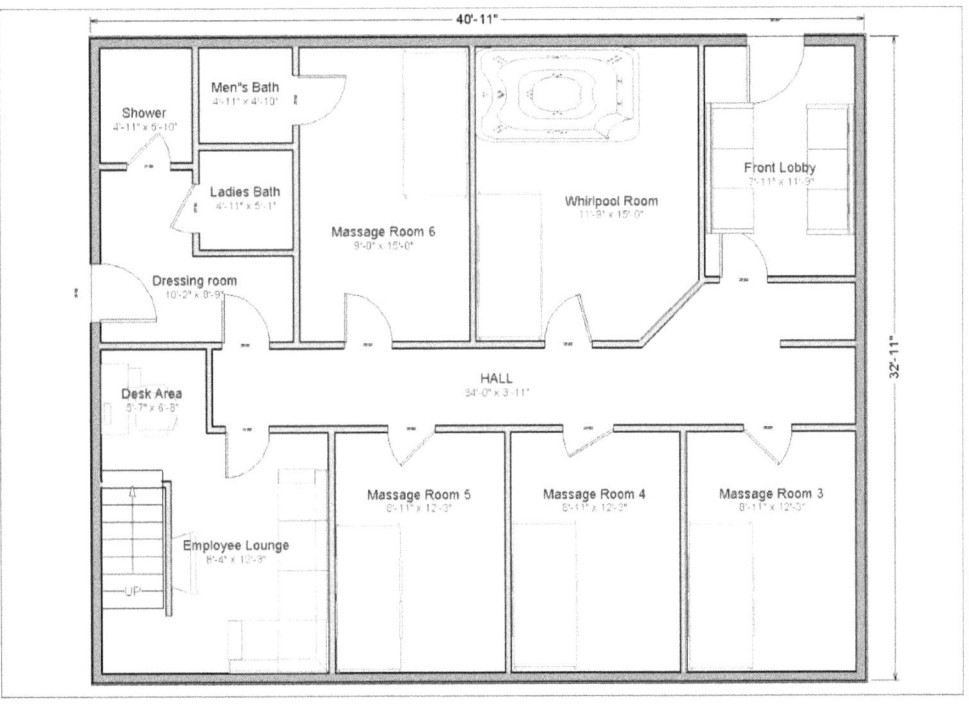

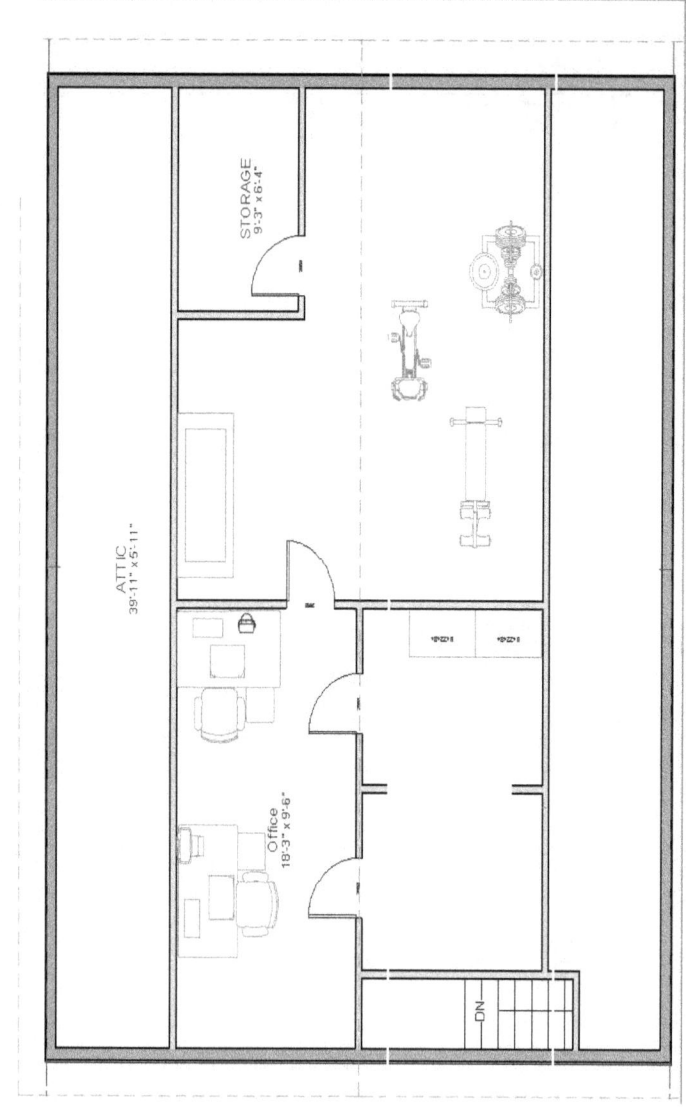

STORAGE
9'-3" x 6'-4"

ATTIC
39'-11" x 5'-11"

Office
18'-3" x 9'-6"

DN

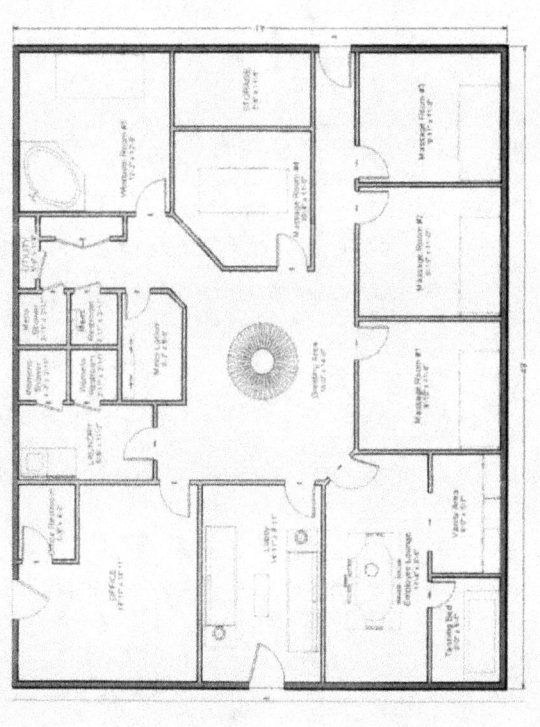

71

Example of Employee's Money Envelope

Employee		Date

Time	Charge Card # Tip Amount on Charge	Total Sales Amount
(example) 1:30pm	Cash	$120.00
2:15pm	Visa 42250065125 $50.00	$170.00
3:20pm	MC 55169751011	$240.00
4:05	Cash	$220.00
	Envelope's Total Sales	$750.00
Employee Initials	Total Enclosed	$750.00

EXAMPLE, "PERSONAL GRID"

EMPLOYEE	M	T	W	TH	F	S	SU	TOTAL
Mary	130	130	370	540	370	off	off	1540.00
Sue	240	off	off	480	720	220 240	370	2030.00
Jane	off	480	480	90	960	370	off	2620.00
Roxanne	370	off	370	240	530	760	off	2270.00
Laura	90	310	180	off	off	1200	240	2020.00
Tabby	480	130	480 130	240	720	720	off	2770.00
Zoey	220	220 480	480	off	1040	960	off	3050.00
Amanda	off	240	260	260	1200	610	off	3050.00
Jessie	off	590	off	90	130 370	820	480	2110.00
Eve	off	off	370	260	780	480	240	2500.00
TOTAL'S	1530	2580	3120	2030	6990	6580	1350	23960.00 23960.00

73

WHITE SHEET   Saturday   DAY   NIGHT DATE   12-24-12

EMPLOYEE	LENGTH OF MASSAGE	MEMBERSHIP NUMBER	DESCRIPTION	TIP	TIME	CHARGE	CASH AMOUNT
Tabby	120	7322	contractor	$25.00	11:15am		$120.00
Amanda	65	4321	engineer	$40.00	2:20pm	$80.00	
Eve	120	5225	attorney	$100.00	5:00pm		$120.00
Sue	65	1234	teacher	$20.00	5:15pm		$65.00
Amanda	90	2468	doctor	$80.00	5:35pm	$120.00	
Eve	65	6789	banker	$30.00	5:45pm		$65.00
Sue	120	3456	insurance	$40.00	5:55pm		$65.00
Tabby	120	1987	state trooper	$70.00	6:00pm	$170.00	
Total's						$370.00	$435.00

Combined total $805.00